U0065798

心・道

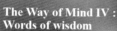

The Way of Mind IV: Words of wisdom

One heart, one mind
Two kinds of love
Three acts of goodness

第四輯

道法師 語錄
Dharma Master
in Tao

目錄

Contents

One heart, one mind :
the marvelous heart, the marvelous
mind of nirvana
Two kinds of love :
love for the earth and love for peace
Three acts of goodness :
wholesome actions of body,
speech, and mind

心道法師一九四八年生，祖籍雲南，幼失依怙，為滇緬邊境孤雛。十三歲隨孤軍撤移來台，十五歲初聞觀音菩薩聖號，有感於觀音菩薩的悲願，以「悟性報觀音」、「吾不成佛誓不休」、「真如度眾生」刺身供佛，立誓

The Way of Mind IV : Words of wisdom
One heart, one mind / Two kinds of love
Three acts of goodness

智慧法語 一心篇

徹悟真理，救度苦難。

　　二十五歲出家後，頭陀行腳歷十餘年，前後在台北外雙溪、宜蘭礁溪圓明寺、莿仔崙墳塔、龍潭公墓和員山周舉人廢墟，體驗世間最幽隱不堪的「塚間修」，矢志修證，了脫生死，覺悟本來。

The Way of Mind IV : Words of wisdom
One heart, one mind / Two kinds of love
Three acts of goodness

無生道場」，展開弘法
度生的佛行事業，為現
代人擘劃成佛地圖。為
了推動宗教共存共榮，
法師以慈悲的華嚴理念
奔走國際，並於二〇〇
一年十一月成立世界宗
教博物館，致力於各種
不同宗教的對話，提昇
對所有宗教的寬容、尊

The Way of Mind IV : Words of wisdom
One heart, one mind / Two kinds of love
Three acts of goodness

規範;「般若期」著重
在明瞭與貫徹空性智
慧;「法華期」著重生
起願力,發菩提心;
「華嚴期」則強調多元
共存、和諧共生,證
入圓滿無礙的境界。

　　近年來,心道法
師以「一心到六度」六
項生活原則,作為普羅

The Way of Mind IV : Words of wisdom
One heart, one mind / Two kinds of love
Three acts of goodness

智慧法語　一心篇

人方便;「五德」正
面、積極、樂觀、愛
心、願力;「六度」
布施、持戒、忍辱、
精進、禪定、智慧。

　　心道法師以禪的
攝心觀照為本、教育
弘法為主軸,用慈悲
願力守護人類心靈,
以世界和平為終生職

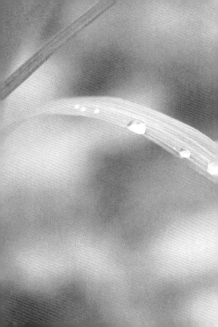

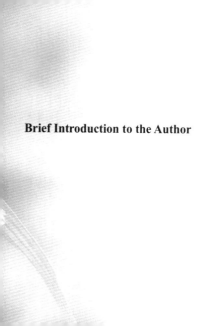

Brief Introduction to the Author

一心・二愛・三好

Born in upper
Myanmar in 1948
to ethnic Chinese
parents of Yunnan
Province, Master
Hsin Tao was left
o r p h a n e d   a n d
impoverished at an
early age. Having

The Way of Mind IV : Words of wisdom
One heart, one mind / Two kinds of love
Three acts of goodness

智慧法語
一心篇

been taken in by
the remnants of
ROC military units
operating along the
border of Yunnan,
China, he was
brought to Taiwan in
1961 when he was 13.
At the age of 15, he

The Way of Mind IV : Words of wisdom
One heart, one mind / Two kinds of love
Three acts of goodness

智慧法語
一心篇

As an offering to
the Buddha, he had
himself tattooed
with the vows
"May I awaken
in gratitude for
the kindness of
Guanyin,""I will
never rest until

during which time he attained deep insight into the meaning of "Only when all beings are liberated, is enlightenment fully attained." Standing on the summit of the

The Way of Mind IV : Words of wisdom
One heart, one mind : Two kinds of love
Three acts of goodness

in Yuanshan, Yilan county.

Having arrived at the Fahua Cave on Fulong Mountain in early 1983, Master Hsin Tao undertook a fast which was to last over two years,

The Way of Mind IV : Words of wisdom
One heart, one mind / Two kinds of love
Three acts of goodness

Ling Jiou Mountain, looking down at the Pacific Ocean, Master Hsin Tao felt great compassion for the suffering of all sentient beings. After his solitary retreat he established

The Way of Mind IV : Words of wisdom
One heart, one mind / Two kinds of love
Three acts of goodness

智慧法語
一心篇

world a proper path
to enlightenment.
In addition,
Master Hsin Tao
strived hard to
gain international
support with the
compassionate spirit
of the Buddhist

Avatamsaka Vision(of the interconnectedness of all beings in the universe), and working for the coexistence and co-prosperity of all religions, completed

The Way of Mind IV : Words of wisdom
One heart, one mind / Two kinds of love
Three acts of goodness

智慧法語
一心篇

the construction
of the Museum of
World Religions in
November 2001.
This Museum
is dedicated to
advancing the cause
of world peace
and a promoting

The Way of Mind IV : Words of wisdom
One heart, one mind / Two kinds of love
Three acts of goodness

智慧法語
一心篇

Tolerance, and Love."
Master Hsin
Tao's vision of
Buddhist education
can be seen in
his "four-stage
training program,"
a systematic and
comprehensive

approach applicable
to both monastics
and lay practitioners
alike to help
them deepen their
practice. Frist comes
the āgama stage,
which centers on
the foundational

The Way of Mind IV : Words of wisdom
One heart, one mind / Two kinds of love
Three acts of goodness
智慧法語 一心篇

teachings of
Buddhism and
the three-fold
practice of morality,
concentration, and
wisdom. The Prajñā
stage emphasizes
the insight into
and practice of

emptiness. The
dharmapuṇḍarīka
stage focuses on
the bodhisattva
p r a c t i c e o f
developing the mind
of enlightenment
through the power
of the vow. Finally,

The Way of Mind IV : Words of wisdom
One heart, one mind / Two kinds of love
Three acts of goodness

智慧法語
一心篇

the avataṃsaka
stage emphasizes
coexistence in
diversity and
focuses on realizing
the ultimate state of
harmony beyond all
obstruction.

In recent years

Master Hsin Tao has been encouraging his disciples to apply the "six principles of spiritual practice" in their daily lives, as a way of implementing his teaching that "Work

The Way of Mind IV : Words of wisdom
One heart, one mind / Two kinds of love
Three acts of goodness
智慧法語 一心篇

is practice; life is
a field of merit."
The one mind is the
marvelous mind
of nirvana. The
two kinds of love
are love for the
earth and love for
peace. The three

acts of goodness are
wholesome actions
of body, speech,
and mind. The
four gifts are joy,
confidence, hope,
and skillful means.
The five virtues:
positive attitude,

The Way of Mind IV : Words of wisdom
One heart, one mind / Two kinds of love
Three acts of goodness
一心篇

zeal, optimism, love, and the power of a vow. The six perfections are generosity, morality, patience, energy, concentration, and wisdom.

Master Hsin Tao

has devoted himself
to propagating the
Dharma through
education, based on
the Chan principle
of concentrating
the mind and
seeing one's
original Buddha-

The Way of Mind IV : Words of wisdom
One heart, one mind / Two kinds of love
Three acts of goodness
一心篇

nature. Through compassion, he makes great efforts to protect and care for all sentient beings. Taking the establishment of world peace as his lifelong

The Way of Mind IV : Words of wisdom
One heart, one mind / Two kinds of love
Three acts of goodness

through Dharma
p r a c t i c e   f o r
generations to come.

一心篇

一心：涅槃妙心

二愛：愛地球、愛和平

三好：身好、口好、意好

One Heart, One Mind

One heart, one mind :
the marvelous heart,
the marvelous mind of nirvana

Two kinds of love :
love for the earth and love for peace

Three acts of goodness :
wholesome actions of body,
speech, and mind

一心

就是涅槃妙心。

The Way of Mind IV : Words of wisdom
One heart, one mind / Two kinds of love
Three acts of goodness

The one heart,
the one mind,
is the marvelous heart,
the marvelous mind of
nirvana.

The Way of Mind IV : Words of wisdom
One heart, one mind / Two kinds of love
Three acts of goodness

智慧法語 心篇

The heart which neither
arises nor ceases is the
marvelous heart of nirvana.

The Way of Mind IV : Words of wisdom
One heart, one mind / Two kinds of love
Three acts of goodness

智慧法語
一心篇

Nirvana is the
appearance of the heart;
the appearance of the heart
is the true form of the
formless.

The Way of Mind IV : Words of wisdom
One heart, one mind / Two kinds of love
Three acts of goodness

智慧法語
一心篇

The marvelous mind, the marvelous heart of nirvana is the goal of the practice.

The spiritual is eternal;
the phenomenal is
temporary.

讓心回家，
回到我們最原始的
根本靈性。

The Way of Mind IV : Words of wisdom
One heart, one mind / Two kinds of love
Three acts of goodness

智慧法語
一心篇

Let the heart return to
its true home,
back to its primordial
spiritual nature.

我們慢慢收回
過去的習氣，
從止觀到達純淨的靈性。

The Way of Mind IV : Words of wisdom
One heart, one mind / Two kinds of love
Three acts of goodness

智慧法語 一 心篇

Gradually overcoming
old habits,
we use the practice of
stopping and seeing to
arrive at our pure
spiritual nature.

把妄念和執著撥開，
讓心回到原點。

The Way of Mind IV : Words of wisdom
One heart, one mind / Two kinds of love
Three acts of goodness

智慧法語
一心篇

Do away with delusion
and attachment;
allow the mind to return
to its source.

locations, including
Waishuangxi in
Taipei, Yuanming
Temple in Yilan,
Chingtzulun Grave
Tower, Longtan
Cemetery, and the
ruins of the frist-
degree Scholar Chou

The Way of Mind IV : Words of wisdom
One heart, one mind / Two kinds of love
Three acts of goodness

Clearly aware from
moment to moment,
we find the source of reality.

The Way of Mind IV : Words of wisdom
One heart, one mind / Two kinds of love
Three acts of goodness

一心篇 智慧法語

Contemplate your
awakened nature;
comprehend your
buddha-nature;
realize your original face.

所有的修行、
所有的止觀，
都是為了
達到空性的連結。

The Way of Mind IV : Words of wisdom
One heart, one mind / Two kinds of love
Three acts of goodness

智慧法語 一心篇

Without contemplation,
liberation remains out
of reach.

觀照自己的覺性，
明白自己的佛性，
證悟自己的本來面目。

The Way of Mind IV : Words of wisdom
One heart, one mind / Two kinds of love
Three acts of goodness

智慧法語
一心篇

All forms of
spiritual practice,
every way of stopping
and seeing—they're all
for arriving at emptiness.

The Way of Mind IV : Words of wisdom
One heart, one mind / Two kinds of love
Three acts of goodness

智慧法語
一心篇

Practicing Buddhism
doesn't mean merely
adopting certain views;
rather, it's a kind of
experiential training
that leads to awakening.

佛法給我們正確的思緒，
也就是正念；
有了正念，
我們才會快樂。

The Way of Mind IV : Words of wisdom
One heart, one mind / Two kinds of love
Three acts of goodness

智慧法語
一心篇

The Buddha's teaching
rectifies our way of
thinking; it teaches us the
right views required
for happiness.

學佛就是放下
一切的緣生緣滅，
回到無我。

The Way of Mind IV : Words of wisdom
One heart, one mind / Two kinds of love
Three acts of goodness

Practicing Buddhism means letting go of everything that arises and ceases dependent on conditions; it's returning to that which is "not-self."

The Way of Mind IV : Words of wisdom
One heart, one mind / Two kinds of love
Three acts of goodness

智慧法語
一心篇

The nature of the mind and
heart neither arises
nor ceases;
it is neither pure nor
impure;
it neither increases nor
decreases.

The Way of Mind IV : Words of wisdom
One heart, one mind / Two kinds of love
Three acts of goodness

智慧法語
一心篇

Only when the heart
remains unmoved
by external conditions
is it possible to end
the cycle of birth and death.

慈悲就是利他成佛，
讓每個人種下菩提種。

The Way of Mind IV : Words of wisdom
One heart, one mind / Two kinds of love
Three acts of goodness

智慧法語
一
心
篇

Compassion means
benefitting others so
that they can awaken,
encouraging others to
plant the seeds of
awakening which grow
into buddhahood.

在生活裡面
用無我去利他，
慈悲才能夠究竟。

The Way of Mind IV : Words of wisdom
One heart, one mind / Two kinds of love
Three acts of goodness

智慧法語
一心篇

By selflessly benefitting others we reach the perfection of compassion.

時時刻刻不離開
覺醒與慈悲，
就能夠靈光、清楚、
智慧一切。

The Way of Mind IV : Words of wisdom
One heart, one mind / Two kinds of love
Three acts of goodness

智慧法語 心篇

Maintaining awareness and
compassion at all times,
we gain insight into
all things.

The Way of Mind IV : Words of wisdom
One heart, one mind / Two kinds of love
Three acts of goodness

智慧法語
一心篇

Compassion means
striving to relieve suffering;
loving kindness means
contemplating with
wisdom.

想出離輪迴，
就要攝心觀照。

The Way of Mind IV : Words of wisdom
One heart, one mind / Two kinds of love
Three acts of goodness

智慧法語
一心篇

Ending the cycle of
birth and death requires
taking hold of the mind
and observing it.

The Way of Mind IV : Words of wisdom
One heart, one mind / Two kinds of love
Three acts of goodness

智慧法語 一心篇

Our spiritual nature
is our buddha-nature;
spiritual practice
means returning to
our spiritual nature.

The Way of Mind IV : Words of wisdom
One heart, one mind / Two kinds of love
Three acts of goodness

智慧法語
一心篇

Returning to our spiritual
nature is the purpose of
Buddhist practice.

覺悟心之道，
就能夠達到一切無礙。

The Way of Mind IV : Words of wisdom
One heart, one mind / Two kinds of love
Three acts of goodness

智慧法語 一心篇

Awakening to the way
of the heart,
we transcend all obstacles.

The Way of Mind IV : Words of wisdom
One heart, one mind / Two kinds of love
Three acts of goodness

智慧法語 心篇

An unconfused mind is an
untainted mind.

安住在寂靜、
安住在無聲、
安住在沒有，
讓我們的心不忙碌。

The Way of Mind IV : Words of wisdom
One heart, one mind / Two kinds of love
Three acts of goodness

智慧法語 一心篇

Peacefully abiding in
silence, no-sound,
and emptiness,
the mind comes to rest.

生滅心不見的時候，
寂靜就出來了。

The Way of Mind IV : Words of wisdom
One heart, one mind / Two kinds of love
Three acts of goodness

智慧法語
一心篇

Silence comes forth
when the heart,
the mind of arising and
ceasing disappears.

回到寧靜，
就會產生無礙的智慧。

The Way of Mind IV : Words of wisdom
One heart, one mind / Two kinds of love
Three acts of goodness

智慧法語 一心篇

Returning to silence,
unobstructed wisdom
arises.

在寂靜的靈覺裡面，
明明白白地去生活。

The Way of Mind IV : Words of wisdom
One heart, one mind / Two kinds of love
Three acts of goodness

智慧法語
一心篇

Abiding in the tranquility of
spiritual awareness,
live with understanding.

The Way of Mind IV : Words of wisdom
One heart, one mind / Two kinds of love
Three acts of goodness

智慧法語 心篇

Listening to silence
without attachment,
allow all thoughts and ideas
to return to emptiness.

The Way of Mind IV : Words of wisdom
One heart, one mind / Two kinds of love
Three acts of goodness

智慧法語
一心篇

In this world of transience,
what's most important is
remaining clearly aware
in the present moment.

在輪迴的勾集裡
放下一切，
無住、無罣、無念。

The Way of Mind IV : Words of wisdom
One heart, one mind / Two kinds of love
Three acts of goodness

智慧法語
一心篇

Letting go of all worldly
pursuits and entanglements,
we experience unobstructed
non-abiding, free of worry.

The Way of Mind IV : Words of wisdom
One heart, one mind / Two kinds of love
Three acts of goodness

智慧法語
一心篇

Having no view is the
proper view.

二愛就是
愛地球、愛和平。

The Way of Mind IV : Words of wisdom
One heart, one mind / Two kinds of love
Three acts of goodness

智慧法語
一心篇

The two kinds of love are
love for the earth and love
for peace.

愛地球是我們生命
共同的方向，
與生命覺醒的出發。

The Way of Mind IV : Words of wisdom
One heart, one mind / Two kinds of love
Three acts of goodness

智慧法語
一心篇

Love for the earth is our
common duty;
it conduces to awakening
to life.

貫徹地球一家，
就要做好慈悲與禪。

The Way of Mind IV : Words of wisdom
One heart, one mind / Two kinds of love
Three acts of goodness

智慧法語 一心篇

Uniting all humanity into
a single family begins with
compassion and meditation.

The Way of Mind IV : Words of wisdom
One heart, one mind / Two kinds of love
Three acts of goodness

The whole universe is a
single community of life.

The Way of Mind IV : Words of wisdom
One heart, one mind / Two kinds of love
Three acts of goodness

We need to respect, accept,
and love all sentient beings.

讓慈悲的種子
彼此串聯,
成為和平的網絡。

The Way of Mind IV : Words of wisdom
One heart, one mind / Two kinds of love
Three acts of goodness
智慧法語
一心篇

Connect the seeds of
compassion into a network
of peace.

The Way of Mind IV : Words of wisdom
One heart, one mind / Two kinds of love
Three acts of goodness

智慧法語
一
心
篇

The road of peace is the
road of friendship
and companionship.

The Way of Mind IV : Words of wisdom
One heart, one mind / Two kinds of love
Three acts of goodness

智慧法語
一心篇

Pacifying the mind and
heart requires Chan
meditation practice.

The Way of Mind IV : Words of wisdom
One heart, one mind / Two kinds of love
Three acts of goodness

Spiritual awakening is what
unleashes our inherent
altruistic love.

用慈悲
化解一切的障礙。

The Way of Mind IV : Words of wisdom
One heart, one mind / Two kinds of love
Three acts of goodness

智慧法語
心篇

Compassion overcomes
all obstructions.

The Way of Mind IV : Words of wisdom
One heart, one mind / Two kinds of love
Three acts of goodness

智慧法語
一心篇

Make the world peaceful and free of strife.

發菩提心，
利益眾生能夠成佛。

The Way of Mind IV : Words of wisdom
One heart, one mind / Two kinds of love
Three acts of goodness

智慧法語
一心篇

Generating the mind of
awakening inspires others
to strive for buddhahood.

Acceptance of others is
born of mutual respect.

The Way of Mind IV : Words of wisdom
One heart, one mind / Two kinds of love
Three acts of goodness

智慧法語 一心篇

Mutual acceptance is the source of peaceful coexistence in diversity.

我們彼此的關係
是共生、相依共存的。

The Way of Mind IV : Words of wisdom
One heart, one mind / Two kinds of love
Three acts of goodness

智慧法語 一心篇

We are bound together by
interdependence.

我們是生命共同體，
哪裡有問題，
我們都能感同身受。

The Way of Mind IV : Words of wisdom
One heart, one mind / Two kinds of love
Three acts of goodness

智慧法語
一心篇

By virtue of
our interconnectedness,
we feel the pain of
others as our own.

積極關懷每一個生命，
引導世界從衝突、對立
走向和諧共生。

We need to be actively
concerned for the welfare
of every single being and
strive to transform conflict
into peace.

The Way of Mind IV : Words of wisdom
One heart, one mind / Two kinds of love
Three acts of goodness
智慧法語 一心篇

All elements of the natural
world are interconnected;
damaging the environment
throws nature out of
balance.

若要找到和平的源頭，
　　就要與自然生態
產生和諧；有了和諧，
就有了多元共生的根據。

The Way of Mind IV : Words of wisdom
One heart, one mind / Two kinds of love
Three acts of goodness

智慧法語
一心篇

If we want to find the source of peace, we need to live in harmony with nature. Harmony with nature reveals the principles of interdependence and peaceful coexistence.

讓地球健康，
人類才能夠永續。

The Way of Mind IV : Words of wisdom
One heart, one mind / Two kinds of love
Three acts of goodness

A healthy planet is a
prerequisite for the
sustainability of mankind.

The Way of Mind IV : Words of wisdom
One heart, one mind / Two kinds of love
Three acts of goodness

智慧法語
一心篇

The three acts of goodness
are wholesome actions of
body, speech, and mind.

身好就是
不殺生、不偷盜、不邪淫

The Way of Mind IV : Words of wisdom
One heart, one mind / Two kinds of love
Three acts of goodness
心篇
智慧法語

In terms of the body,
this means refraining from
killing, stealing,
and sexual misconduct.

口好就是
不妄語、不兩舌、
不惡口、不綺語。

The Way of Mind IV : Words of wisdom
One heart, one mind / Two kinds of love
Three acts of goodness

智慧法語
一心篇

In terms of speech, this
means refraining from
lying, divisive speech,
harsh speech,
and frivolous speech.

The Way of Mind IV : Words of wisdom
One heart, one mind / Two kinds of love
Three acts of goodness

一心篇

In terms of mind, this
means refraining from
greed, hatred, and delusion.

The Way of Mind IV : Words of wisdom
One heart, one mind / Two kinds of love
Three acts of goodness

智慧法語
一心篇

We need to plant
wholesome seeds of body,
speech, and mind.

When the mind and
speech are wholesome,
we naturally engage in
wholesome actions.

一心・二愛・三好

存好心、
做好事、
說好話，
就是解脫的法門。

The Way of Mind IV : Words of wisdom
One heart, one mind / Two kinds of love
Three acts of goodness

智慧法語 一心篇

Engaging in wholesome
actions of body, speech,
and mind, we pass through
the gate of liberation.

The Way of Mind IV : Words of wisdom
One heart, one mind / Two kinds of love
Three acts of goodness

智慧法語
一心篇

Practicing the three forms
of wholesome action is
a way of honing one's
character.

常常在三寶上
覺醒、解脫、清淨，
就能夠
身好、口好、意好。

The Way of Mind IV : Words of wisdom
One heart, one mind / Two kinds of love
Three acts of goodness

智慧法語
一心篇

Reaching awakening, liberation and purity of spirit through constant recollection of the Triple Gem leads to wholesome actions of body, speech, and mind.

The Way of Mind IV : Words of wisdom
One heart, one mind / Two kinds of love
Three acts of goodness

智慧法語
一心篇

Praising that which is
praiseworthy generates
wholesome karma.

一心・二愛・三好

要度眾生，要有善業；
要成就，也要有善業。

The Way of Mind IV : Words of wisdom
One heart, one mind / Two kinds of love
Three acts of goodness

智慧法語
一心篇

Bringing the practice to
fruition and inspiring
others to do the same
requires a sufficient store of
wholesome karma.

從善業裡
做到清淨解脫，
從清淨解脫裡
去發菩提心。

The Way of Mind IV : Words of wisdom
One heart, one mind / Two kinds of love
Three acts of goodness

智慧法語
一心篇

Good karma leads to the purity and liberation of spirit wherein is generated bodhicitta.

累積善緣，
就會得到快樂與成功

The Way of Mind IV : Words of wisdom
One heart, one mind / Two kinds of love
Three acts of goodness

智慧法語
一
心
篇

Establishing wholesome affinities brings happiness and success.

不要把
成佛的善業停擺，
要反覆觀照，
慈悲一切。

The Way of Mind IV : Words of wisdom
One heart, one mind / Two kinds of love
Three acts of goodness

智慧法語
一心篇

Don't let your good karma
go to waste;
attain buddhahood through
the application of diligent
contemplation and universal
compassion.

The Way of Mind IV : Words of wisdom
One heart, one mind / Two kinds of love
Three acts of goodness

智慧法語
一心篇

When generosity
becomes second nature,
happiness is sure to follow.

The Way of Mind IV : Words of wisdom
One heart, one mind / Two kinds of love
Three acts of goodness

智慧法語
一心篇

Transforming the power
of karma into the power
of a vow,
appiness naturally follows.

累積福德
就是實實在在
去幫助有苦難的人。

沉迷欲望就是貪，
敵對殺戮就是瞋，
執迷不悟就是癡。

The Way of Mind IV : Words of wisdom
One heart, one mind / Two kinds of love
Three acts of goodness

Greed begets covetousness
and addiction;
hatred begets enmity
and violence;
delusion begets confusion.

The Way of Mind IV : Words of wisdom
One heart, one mind / Two kinds of love
Three acts of goodness

智慧法語
一心篇

The antidotes for greed, hatred, and delusion are generosity, compassion, and wisdom.

物質世界的任何東西，
都是因果的呈現。

The Way of Mind IV : Words of wisdom
One heart, one mind / Two kinds of love
Three acts of goodness

智慧法語
一心篇

All material objects are
manifestations of the
principle of cause and
effect.

The Way of Mind IV : Words of wisdom
One heart, one mind / Two kinds of love
Three acts of goodness

智慧法語
一
心篇

Cause and effect is
the central tenet of the
Buddha's teaching.

我們今生可以做的，
就是把不好的因果轉好，
把好的因果繼續耕耘。

The Way of Mind IV : Words of wisdom
One heart, one mind / Two kinds of love
Three acts of goodness

一心篇

In this very lifetime it's possible to transform bad karma into good karma, and to continue cultivating more good karma.

The Way of Mind IV : Words of wisdom
One heart, one mind / Two kinds of love
Three acts of goodness

智慧法語
一心篇

Use everything is life to cultivate the mind and eradicate bad habits.

The Way of Mind IV : Words of wisdom
One heart, one mind / Two kinds of love
Three acts of goodness
一心篇
智慧法語

Never miss an opportunity
to create wholesome
relations with others
to perfect your karmic
affinities.

從善業裡面去發願，
從惡業裡面去度苦。

The Way of Mind IV : Words of wisdom
One heart, one mind / Two kinds of love
Three acts of goodness

智慧法語
一心篇

Wholesome karma is the basis for making a vow; unwholesome karma is the basis for transcending suffering.

If you want to be reborn
in the pure land,
you have to practice
boundless generosity
and serve others selflessly.

隨身智慧寶典

智慧法語系列①～④輯

心之道

閱讀心道法師語錄，
可以讓個人在日常生活中如實觀照；
一天一法語，啟開智慧「心」生活。

The Way of Mind I~IV:
Words of wisdom

心道法師 語錄
By Dharma Master
Hsin Tao

靈鷲山般若書坊

第一輯

修慧篇 Cultivate Wisdom

修心篇 Cultivate Mind

修行篇 Cultivate Spirituality

第二輯

Compassion 慈悲篇

Joyful Giving 喜捨篇

第三輯

律己篇 Self-restraint

止觀篇 Tranquility and insight

願力篇 The force of a vow

證果篇 Realization

第四輯

One Heart, One Mind 一心篇

The Six Perfections 六度篇

心之道智慧法語 第四輯

一心篇——一心／二愛／三好

心道法師語錄

總　策　劃：釋了意
主　　　編：洪淑妍
責任編輯：林美伶
英文翻譯：甘修慧
英文審校：Dr. Maria Reis Habito
美術設計：黃偉哲
發　行　人：黃虹如
出版發行：財團法人靈鷲山般若文教基金會附設出版
劃撥帳戶：財團法人靈鷲山般若文教基金會附設出版
劃撥帳號：18887793
地　　　址：23444 新北市永和區保生路2號21樓
電　　　話：(02) 2232-1008
傳　　　真：(02) 2232-1010
網　　　址：www.093books.com.tw
讀者信箱：books@ljm.org.tw
法律顧問：永然聯合法律事務所
印　　　製：東豪印刷事業有限公司
初版一刷：2018年8月
定　　　價：新台幣220元（1套2冊）
I S B N：978-986-96539-3-0
總　經　銷：飛鴻國際行銷股份有限公司

he Way of Mind IV : Words of wisdom
)ne Heart, One Mind—One heart, one mind / wo kinds of love / Three acts of goodness

Vords of Dharma Master Hsin Tao

eneral Planer : Ven.Liao Yi Shih

ditor in Chief : Hung, Shu-yen

ditor in Charge : Lin, Mei-ling

nglish translator : Ken Kraynak

nglish Proofreading : Dr. Maria Reis Habito

rt Editor : Huang, Wei-jer

ublisher : Huang, Hung-ju

ublished by and The postal service is allocated :
ing Jiou Mountain Press, Ling Jiou Mountain Prajna
ultural and Educational Foundation

ccount number : 18887793

ddress : 21F., No.2, Baosheng Rd., Yonghe Dist., New
aipei City 23444, Taiwan (R.O.C.)

el : (02)2232-1008 / Fax : (02)2232-1010

Vebsite : www.093books.com.tw

-mail : books@ljm.org.tw

egal Consultant : Y. R. Lee & Partners Attorneys at Law

rinting : Sunrise Printing Co., Ltd.

he First Printing of the First Edition : August, 2018

ist Price : NT$ 220 dollars (Two-Manual Set)

SBN :978-986-96539-3-0

istributor : Flying Horn International Marketing Co., Ltd.

國家圖書館出版品預行編目(CIP)資料

心之道智慧法語. 第四輯 / 洪淑妍主編.-- 初版
-- 新北市：靈鷲山般若出版, 2018. 08
冊 ； 公分
ISBN 978-986-96539-3-0 (全套：精裝)

1. 佛教說法 2. 佛教教化法

225. 4   107011669